W9-AEF-377

Falling

FALLING

Daniel Hughes

Copper Beech Press

Providence 1979

ACKNOWLEDGEMENTS

Some of these poems have appeared in

The New York Times
The New York Times Book of Verse
Michigan Signatures
The Windsor Review
The Ontario Review
Anon
Riverrun
The Mad River Review
The Wayne Review

ISBN: 0-914278-24-X

Copper Beech Press
Box 1852/Brown University
Providence, Rhode Island 02912

This book was made possible by a grant from the National Endowment for the Arts in Washington, D.C., a Federal agency.

Typeset by Ed Hogan/Aspect Composition
1105 Broadway, Somerville, Mass. 02144

TABLE OF CONTENTS

To Edwin Honig

ONE

FALLING

Walking on basketballs to Woodward,
the soft uncertain feet, "Touch,
come down, settle, anchor your ankles,
for God's sake, the ground will hold you!",

but it will not rise or open,
nor any hand or hook or clutch
of circumstance beyond belief
make a next step the likely one.

And you will run, and you will fall,
not as you think, the Fall Voluptuous,
drifting like pollen down,
nor the Fall Pensive, pondered well,

but the Fall Stunning, running for the bus—
O tumble like a pin pulled free!—
and again you're glad to be flat,
as the air is let out of everything.

ELPENOR

Elpenor, my self, my guile, my alter fool,
neither in battle, nor in bed worth much,
and in brains always lagging behind—at school
to crafty Odysseus—when you climbed

to Circe's roof, what did you hope to find there?
A smirkless moon, one swelling, friendly star,
a god on his way home to Olympus
who might tell you you were not what you are?

Elpenor, waked by the strong voices embarking
for Hades, the Sorrowing Waters, the Gloom,
and down the ladder with a pratfall crashing,
sorry to take that short-cut to your doom,

we, the clumsy, the clownish, salute you,
for never shall you rot in Circe's sty.
We understand you and hope cruel Homer did.
We will fall with you, Cousin, when we die.

LIVES OF THE CAESARS

1. Caesar's Dream

Bald Caesar, thrashing like a tuna, awoke
and pushed the woman from him, though she clung
like the rank greens of autumn, like a swamp
clutching whole armies of retreat—
bald Caesar, shaking like a stag, arose
and struck the gong that brought a wise man running.

Equipment at the ready, snails, gut of lamb,
nail of hawk and toad, intestines of the air,
he spread them before Caesar. "I dreamt
that I was raping my mother, my own flesh,
that she gave birth to monsters with twelve heads,
all of whom then slew us in our beds."

"Ah, Caesar," the soothsayer said, "I've got it!
Have no fear of playing Oedipus or worse;
that dream was more a blessing than a curse.
That was Mother Earth you mastered, can't you see?
The whole world lies waiting for your sword;
the dream that woke you was of victory."

Was Caesar satisfied? The chronicle is mute,
but turning to his couch and whore again,
some shade of terror must have lingered there,
some disaster that might bring his line to ground.
For while her nails streaked down his back,
he wondered what he did there, and how the world was found.

2. Tiberius

Nibbling and nibbled to prove that he exists,
the tiresome, licentious pool, that dull man,
dullest of the Caesars, once scheming
for the call, the chance to try at God,
he, too, started with the best of intentions.

They all did: decrees to simplify the law,
decrees to complicate the marriage tie,
decrees to clarify decrees, and he wrote
to the Senate, "You'll never know what I'll become,"
and refused to be called "Father of his Country."

He became what he had to, what he always was.
Seleucus, like Charles Van Doren, cheated
and had to die; Mallonia stabbed herself,
recalling his antics in bed. At last, Capri
put out its salmon tongue, our Great Good Place.

Here they come! the *spintriae,* swimming toward him
like champions from Yale, record-minded,
sleek, single, breasting the current of his demand,
cunning dolphins pink in a pawky pool—
proving he is Caesar, that he stands in wet water.

3. Caligula in the Classroom

At the board, listing three facts on Wordsworth,
his back blocks them from this surprising sight:
lips hung slack, eyes bugged free as bursten grapes,
nor can they guess how many hills he's leveled
in that eyelash, Caligula at work.

Best not to know. Best for himself, too, not
to recognize the wide range of his empire
when they spend ten minutes scratching a quiz,
or longer on a sly exam; it's then the lions
charge into the Circus, their climacteric come.

And best not to brood too much on how he'll end,
in some dull corner of the quad, set upon
by loyalties he thought unquestionable:
dying hard, stuck with all his jokes, bled white
by inadequate preparation.

4. Nero at the Morgue

Mother, why did you die so hard?
I planned the boat to drown you in,
built to bend at the proper time,
to fold you like a fan that tipped,
doubled, caught, ensconced in sea,
and down you'd go gulping, with cries
no god could catch, so welded were you.

It failed. But what scheme kept you going,
dallying, unwilling to die?
Didn't my statue scare you silly,
that gigantic pool twit your nerves
when you came to doubtful supper
in my Golden House?

I'll never understand you. Look,
your limbs show first dapplings of decay,
the blue veins blotched to yellow,
and I must admit a puffiness
I never saw in the old days.
How much my foresight has saved us both!
I am the doer of everyman's dream.

5. Lost Page from Suetonius

Of course, I envied them. What made them tick?
And how can I go on with my researches
knowing they were really no more sick
than I am, rummaging through Rome for scandal?

These family trees, like hairy vines, appal.
Yet all the portents only remind us
that our mothers, too, saw eagles fall,
and heaved their wombs to gods that never came.

How stale these pages are that put down
deeds I never dared, wishes that find
only *others* on the flaming town!
Posterity's treat can never be my own.

Suetonius, the never deified,
Suetonius, the hardly edified,
poor Suetonius, folding up his scroll,
knowing unacted deeds take the greatest toll.

EMPIRE FALLING NIGHT

1.
(Insomnia)

I am falling through my skin as the Roman Empire, 1400 years down, went skidding to Goth and Vandal and Hun. Someone in the temple will not watch; someone in the square is waving. I am handing over the optima spolia, the chalice, my piece of the True Cross, John's third head, the treasury even to its smallest shining flake. I know the hordes are here, dragging their gods through the desert. I smell their big horses. Insane with surrender, I run to meet their hairy chieftains. Goth! Vandal! Hun! We were only happy for a day; our tired gates sag forward at your shout... No. There never was an Empire. Dull provinces bestir. I hear the first wheels of someone else's dream.

2.
(Poet)

I am that second Julian
who never kissed the Christian Cross
but peered into old prophecy.

Attend! Attend! Even *my* hands
might balance the blue globe
though the white altars keep settling.

I need all the luck
I ever prayed for in your temple, Terminus.
I need justice and the Serpent's dream. . .

Mad engineers tear out the foundations
and holy Martin howls his monks
upon the bright images.

3.
(Soldier)

Lost in the Persian desert of our will,
my troops mutinous and grey with despair,
I cut taut skins for our river crossing
and stared at the Yellow Tigris, and sat down.
O sophist of Antioch, you got me into this,
believing in gods and the Caesars,
cleaning off temples for the first notions.
Now we wait in sand that blows our eyes out
and the silent Immortals will not come.

4.
(Slice of Life)

Petrus Flaminius, pontifex maximus,
bare-assed, awesome-assed,
took off for the Palatine hill,

and we felt the full seriousness,
the very hug of life again,
to see his flapping penis and daft eye.

The bishops chased him, robes held high.

5.
(To the Readers of Signs)

Look up grey beards and squint my life in order!
I waited so long for your dry report
but only saw your sockets scooped by boiling tears.
O you never knew which way *one* bird was going,
and now the skies are shutting down their lights,
and rank black beasts are calling from our shoulders.

6.
(The Platonic Philsophers Back from Persia)

But it was nothing; it was worse.
So back we came to the border,
and lived there, seven shy thinkers,
Diogenes, Isidore, Simplicius,

Elalius, two others, and I.
It was the smell of the unburied
hied us home. *Live small and in between.*
Let the solitude of your patience

blow your works away. Ask nothing
of the one king or of the other.
We were right to end philosophy.
You have to dig us from the dark.

7.
(Empire Falling Night)

Yes, like you, I was the last emperor of Rome.
The golden eagles on my shoes confirm it.
Lift me out of this salad of corpses
and cut my head off; it still sways like a stem
too full of schemes and shy battalions.
I begged a Christian to sever it clean,
that vegetable of hopes to go bumping down
spread under the horses' hooves—who would know?
Who could prove that Rome ever fell, ever was,
was only a ruck of meat under a charging heel?
But now I will get a tiresome burial
and hoarse mercies will tell lies upon my lips.

8.
(Aubade)

Cathedral to mosque, the day begun!
The wound on its way drives a rose within
and its petals drip invasion wide.
O Patriarch asleep, the hordes are busy,
janizaries of death-straw, death-strum!
Take your dream away; tell no one your god,
In the dark build your secret Rome.

TWO

BIRTHDAY

"Nothing can prevent madness."
—Stendhal

Not the Pincian, the entry to Milan,
or Cimarosa's moony pledge,
will serve to keep you on the edge
of fineness, stoke you warm again.

The day is lost, and the missed beat.
Have I been a clever man, prone
to speak the lesser lies, but groan
in private, mumbling of retreat?

Grow up, and Beyle illusion out!
That dazzling will was all the joke
of a cooling heart afraid to croak—
And "God's last license" is the gout.

Not the Pincian, the years you've had,
like San Gimignano's coffined towers
stacked in a stale defense—hours
of dullness!—not lucky to be mad.

DEBRIS

1

My wife's brain crashing about the kitchen
like the crockery we dropped when told to move,
disturbs my thought, as slowly, from A to A′,
I muse on an old hunger. Dear Clio,
as you step across the fallen cups, bring
me the bright atlases, Rand McNally's ways–
I feel a connection coming.

2

Softly in the left gnarled bone of my head
a memory lifts, like a quick lost hand
at a party: a pretty girl who soothed your palm
when introduced but went home early–
with your friend.

Do you remember the feast of life?
Are you only a dirty monk below the salt?

3
(A Renaissance Portrait)

Federigo da Montefeltro! Lord!
(Was it you on *The Untouchables*,
and always in profile to hide your missing eye?)

Piero set you above the Marchesan waters,
man of strength, musing on the fabled captains,
who made the randy Venetians cry halt,
your intellect swelling the battalions–

who lunched unguarded in the open air,
and always met your enemy full view.

Though you kept no poet's court, nor even read them,
I'm here, your courtier with lance at thigh,
moderate in my needs, easy of speech,
all *sprezzatura* and laughing Italian sun!

The Signoria begs our services
as we ride out—*"Dio vi mantegna, signori!"*—
chatting of the *Ethics.*

Vespasiano knew you, and describes your lovely bindings.

4

(*Reculer pour mieux sauter*)

The veined full boot of Italy on the wall,
a fetishist's delight, the major roads
like scars streaking leather, like those old charts
in my father's white embalming room,
one for the lymph, one for the path of blood,
the weary red and green—no organ to be seen.

Red man, you suddenly swarm to speak your bubble!
My lymph is greening, the pink tongue blisters!
Clipped head, hair-breadth nose, meat-rotten cheek,
the mouth agape where your torrents gathered,
as though you'd make one dripping, final plea—
I must get up to plot our shrieking free.

5

The one hundred and seventy-five ways to make love,
known to a legless guru of Tibet
and Enrico Molinari of New York,
would take this poem further than I need to go.

On Woodward, the fumes rise, the poisons clamor,
the gassed pedestrians remember air.

A flickering "Walk" tempts their broken feet.
I cannot move; my will chokes back on "Wait."

So: standing, sitting, kneeling, upside down,
vaginal, oral, rectal, intra-mammilary,
by letter, by telegram, at the window,
on the freeway, inside the Houston Dome,

there is Love! And now the "Walk" is shining
like the friendly eyes of my lost father.
I will not be crushed on this corner of my life!
I will cross the avenue and start this ancient poem.

IN FLORENCE

In Florence, more gallery than town,
where the vague, stamped faces of the colleges at home
throng the streets like *putti* on a tomb,
I saw the fresh editions moan, *"Marilyn e Morte!"*
"Marilyn, Addio!" and sat down
to translate the first Italian I would read.

The bells at noon put on their pretty news,
the cake cathedral sang. Near Dante's house,
I watched the cameras glut their easy eyes
and felt all Florence preening to be seen.—
Mourning should deck your doors; the world had lost a queen.

More moved by this than by the fustian Medici
was proof enough the traveller would not look,
that all this packing out of history
was truer, cleaner, better in a book,
and no memorials would ever last
like newsprint on the street.

Yet, Michelangelo, come—sculpt a tomb
in your best unfinished style; pull a body
from marble finer than Carrara's best—
then ship it west.

She was our pet, an apparition we had dreamt.
Firenze was never so blonde, so innocent.

HE IS DREAMING MY LIFE

He is dreaming my life; I see him pass
on frantic highways with storm signals up;
I see him turning in cafeterias
with a dried-out bun, a softly smoking cup.

He is dreaming my life: a pervert on the prowl,
trick handles on his roadster to keep me in;
I see him on a twilit lakefront,
tensing the board with his chesty, brainless grin.

He is dreaming my life: I see him stand
in galleries blocking the one Vermeer;
I see him sag at all the damp parades,
then stiffen like a soldier when the flag comes near.

Who are you? What will you say when me meet?
Which one of us is carrying the knife?
Stay off the street! Keep out of public johns!
Fly to the moon—you are dreaming my life.

WAGNERIANA

1

Isolde stays grim for the whole performance.
The deep oppression of the great Wagnerian chord
never lets in a laugh of understanding.
She's down in death's obsidian the whole time.

No good weather, no romp in careless sun,
or clumsy kiss or casual bite of apple.
Isolde's a night-person, becoming Brunnhilde
beneath her cerements of pomp and despair.
Her music is thicker than Victoria's dresses
once glimpsed at Kensington. You ran to the light—
but the love-death locked you in its indoor final hymn.

2

When Auden died a friend played Siegfried's funeral march
and embarrassed and overwhelmed everyone there.
He'd asked for a hero's funeral,
but *that* hero?
When I first heard that music I thought I was a giant
trudging across a decimated landscape
of parents, friends, and enemies all wonderfully dead.

You feel the upward tug, chest inflating to Valhalla,
you sense your coffin building its permanence—
you listen tensely, wishing to be well.

3
(Tristan Beserk)

Not when I was the leper, but the lover,
but I won't tell you what I did
because you know, hypocrite voyeur,
the extremes I went to—everyone knows!

Why not remember my many feats of strength,
dragon-slaying, my clever trick on Gandin,
my late surprising birth, my way with the harp—
no, none of this, not even my sad name
and how well it sets to any music:
Triss-tan! Triss-tan!—such things won't please you.
Always the Cave of Lovers, the Love-Death,
and your egregious sniffing of the potion.

Well, they have always followed me: Gottfried,
Thomas, Wagner, and you dear jealous reader.
Yes, what we did was extraordinary,
Yes, we were out of our skulls.
You know what I did and you hate me for it.

You suspect I *sublimed* myself. I did.

MILORD

"Greece on the Ruins of Missolonghi."—isn't that Byron's arm
crushed by a block? and why's that girl standing there?
Poor Byron, to come to this, writing arm witless, numb.
It wasn't worth it, but Teresa shocking the salon
with "mio Byron!" was worth it, and your letter to Moore:
"Good night or rather morning. It is four
and the dawn gleams over the Grand Canal and unshadows the Rialto."
That was worth it. But that girl? She's history, milord,
and history is never worth it. We know that in Detroit.
Henry Ford said, "History is bunk."—and helped to make it so.

I dream. I am making a movie, *The Last Gondola,*
and you are dangling your club-foot in the Canal.
I tug your memoirs from the mud and read them greedily
while our weary harmless shark-head slides to sea.
Everyone knows that Venice was too grand, improbable,
but "damme, it's life," expensive, grand, dissolving.
The last thing I saw was the dome of the *Salute*
wilting like a flower too long in the rain.

THE DEATH OF ADAM

"Line up for the photograph," he said.
"Arrange yourselves in pairs, or singly.
Participate; or stand alone,
but know you are glorious witness,
you accumulate; forever,
they'll want to know what I found to say."

So we came. I took off my clothes
and posed nimbly above him,
leaning, an athlete on my staff,
back to the camera, left buttock
held fetchingly out. My wife came near,
draped to listen, a sybil in trance,
who looked and sighed down into him,
her eyes sliding from the lens.
My father in his old mock strength
leaned next to me–Ciceronian–
frowning as he was told.

Was that old crone our Mother Eve?
Yes, surely she belonged in the picture!
Come in, come over, old woman,
shuffle into your dignity–
the Sunday editions will dry your tears!
Unsure of her hands, she at last
cupped his deaf right ear and coaxed him
to hear the sea he'd never named.
We were ready. Even our necks
found grandest outlines to sustain,
and we were made beyond the day
to stand erect at evening.

For twenty minutes we held fast
and watched his gums lift and fall,

lift and fall, as an ant moves under a crumb.
I felt my armpits gush; lips crack;
the slow, stagey, burnt-out Eden.

A sudden flash singed him beyond words.

THREE

ADVENTURE

Etna's active again,
and, into it, out of it,
come Empedocles, Matthew Arnold,
and Monica Vitti.
You remember the last scene of *L'Avventura*
when she strokes the hair of the faithless Ferzetti
who's sobbing his wretched heart out
while Etna smokes in the distant purest void?
I'm heading there now. I've climbed Fuji,
why can't I simplify myself into Etna
and find Monica there, dolorosa,
lithe and beautiful and forgiving?

FOR SO MANY

For so many Italy is the edge of the mind,
never to be hauled to its center
where it would look like the place you started from,
lumpen, grey, dissolving.

There are two slabs of time that never meet
and it's not that you dream one and wake the other—
they are just there, without connection or remorse.
The mind sits between them, with least wanting, least will.

This is the hour of the paraplegic, the thalidomide child.
If you reach out, someone will be glad to see you use your spoon.
If you get up, you will be wildly applauded.
But Italy stays there, rolling slowly backward, furry with distance.

TWIN CITIES

If I had never seen Florence would Detroit be possible?
Bureaucrats and businessmen Ren-Cen their garbage as *twin* cities,
but the Florence I saw remains a long sharp dream in my mind.

This picture by Gauffier of the young Englishman, Penrose,
is painful if you pick at its small assertion:
he sits above a sketch-book and pencil he never used;
he looks from the Boboli Gardens in high assumption
of his worth—that English manner so out of fashion now.
Well, he was just young, son of an obscure 18th-century poet—

he kept this picture with him all his life,
hung on the wall of his parsonage at home.
Life went by; he must have looked at it from time to time.
Now it comes to rest dejectedly on this page in Detroit;
its Florentine soft ochre fades each time I look at it.

MUSEO ARCHEOLÓGICO

We *are* helpless and life's a dream all right.
Think of your friends too walking out of their lives
and certainly walking out of yours. Goodbye!
I can't believe it. The names go first or
the pressure of a hand, taste of mouth and
we become our own small dig: the heart's a potsherd.

I admire those Etruscan scholars
who imagine the lost cities of Etruria.
I love the Venus in the Villa Giulia
coming toward me with wide smile, accepting hips,
easy to know it seems, but goddess still.
I remember her better than you for all you did.

Well, I'm planning another museo archeologico.
Heads of lovers will be there, knuckles of enemies,
and a few ingenious panoramic scenes of our best days.
There'll be a great case of letters sent and unsent.
Their cipher's missing, the hand's unreadable,
but there's beauty in that odd lost scrawl beyond sense.

MACHIAVELLI POEMS

1
Machiavelli Watches Savonarola Twist in the Wind

Something about him I admired for all that.
I hate to see him such a flammable rag doll.
Soon he'll go up like any page of broken promises.
He wanted too much—he anguished the wrong people—
but I will see his fierce cowled head for a long time to come.
I puzzle out his lesson; I keep my back to the wind.

2
Machiavelli Falls in Love with Cesare Borgia

I suppose these days it looks like that,
though, God knows, I kept my head when I was with him.
Do you find fault in Remirro d'Orco cut in two,
beside his pieces, a piece of wood and a knife?
The people were "stunned and satisfied." Did they need more?
But Valentino had bad luck, as he told me himself.
I don't like to think of him sick in the Vatican.
I'll have to wait for his wonder to grow in my mind.
He'll become my wish; I'll be his dark swift mastery.

3
Machiavelli Snares Thrushes on his Farm

The poet wants me to be Papageno, bird-cage on my head,
but I'm serious about these thrushes
and snare them with my own hands, and sing no silly tune.
I'm up at dawn, the bird-lime prepared to grease
the twigs on which they're caught, stuck, like thought deferred.
Even when I dress in courtly splendor to read the classics,
the lime smears my fingers. O ancient men,
the disputes we have over *cricca* and trich-trach!
But my mind's not moldy; I'm making my Fate ashamed.

4

Machiavelli Scolds the Author for his Lack of Interest in Politics

What else is there? Women? You need them, you have them,
 it's *nothing*.
Books? I'm very bookish, but their consoling faraway pages
 sadden.
I'm afraid you're the worst type, creature of powerless power,
navel-gazer, timid as a swift and as quickly gone—
No, don't say it! I see the wry, pedantic smile, the wan paradox
forming on your lips to impress only others like yourself.
You're about to say, "In truth, Machiavelli was a poet!"
There—happy with yourself, tickled with your phrasing?
The person I'd least like to live in exile with is you.
You love me more than you will admit; there is no *virtu* in you.

5

What is Art? What is Man?

Leonardo's Vitruvian man gives me the willies.
Scissored, cramped in the bondage of himself,
he would break out, become a newt, a fiery star.

Is there no way out of these damned proportions men seem
 to prefer?
I never see this nude poor thing that I don't feel like praying.

FOUR

BEFORE THE FLOOD

1

The Ache of Gold

The ache of gold, the empty chair
hugged by the brawny fathers of the Church,
the canopy whose bellying curve
unmakes debate—these fill no life.

You are the kitten in Trajan's markets,
starving on first sight—you are Poverty.
You grow so light, so careless now,
you drift through the piazza like a spilled-out pod.

Days were to accumulate, nights refresh,
head like a warrior's—O ringing ears!—
you ran to seal the exits shut,
but let the sun drench you to silence...

In San Clemente Mithra hides
like a hard pea in the stomach.
The corridors are wet, grimly shown.
The small figure in the damp is you.

Rome

2

This City's Square

This city's square leans with human warmth.
Up and down, you walk the tilt and hum,
enormous shell of touch, of thought.
The Campo frets on an old defeat.

Pain is the essence of such places.
Where hope had been, ambition,
the moment of Montaperti, say,
your life's triumphal standard struck—

but the awkward drum of the *contrade,*
the stutter on the tongue to silence
and the missed relation—O traitor!—
and not to know, never to know,

why you came here, who you were.
Yet the galleries are full of faces
lit by an art of permanent gold.
Be happy; take the hands of those you love.

Siena

3

Jets Over Siena

i

Jets over Siena tense the mind,
spoil the soft dispersal of cafes,
where the beautiful English blonde
laughs at her lover through the afternoon.

News nudges in: Vietnam,
the mad sniper in his eyrie,
the nurse-killer missing one,
but each comes medicated like a pill

you don't have to take. The jet-stream
spends itself, oh, far, far away.
The azure drops like a massive door
shut by the Piccolominis on the world.

ii

Dear Lello, "the seriousness
that nature puts in all her works"
is yours now, more solemn than you thought
when you wrote those words to Bosanquet in 1922.

I watch you at table grope for speech,
galantuomo still, your black eyes
searching us for social clues,
until, weary of all translation, you wander off.

More than newsprint spills Siena out
to the old harsh mornings of our homes.
Old man, more delicate than all,
seeing you, I would that we believed in life.

Something to believe in? A phrase
that unabashed? we can be that naked?
Those airplanes were flying blind,
cancelled in the illusory Italian blue.

Siena

4

rittrato d'ignoto e sua moglie

A cloud slices the moon, withdraws. We are alone.
Such a long time for this clarity to emerge!
Sounds damp down. The heavy traffic starts to be
a common hum like breath, and the precise trot
of the horses on the pavement reassures.

The time for honesties has come, our sought fresh weather.
Above San Miniato, the moon does not blink.
This year the Arno is full enough for drinking deep,
and such simplicity seizes me, I babble
to the future like an almanac pressed in green and gold.

For this is the year of harvest, our bodies brown
with fulfillment, the tongue set to its stern meters:
Go love another who takes your fancy like a purse!
O spendthrift order! We are that universal man!
Such economy humbles me, and presses lips all 'round.

You have gone in. Did you know these words were coming?
Did you see me starting engines, oiling up for lies?
You have gone in. Myself to myself swells such a farce
that the hills, the towers, the groaning walls fall down.
Brunelleschi's dome is a wen upon the night.

Florence

5

Satellites

The antennae cross in inner space,
gently, gently, the remotest chance
hurled from the void to the void:
adrift, irresolute, tender.

And who could see their silences,
plot the slow, weighted grappling of their touch?
The signals come back like footsteps
muffling to the imagined plain.

We know they split without injury;
we know they will not cross again.
Would violence have left a sign,
like crumpled cars? Yet the air

is sweeter now, only the air
breathes what they were, what they did.
The polar cap shudders in the mind,
spreads like an unexpected bruise.

Florence

6

More Frescoes

That gesture made without thought, in elegance,
all youth, the beautiful Renaissance boy,
peering from the crowd to smirk: "I'm here, I'm here,
there's nothing in my life but joy!"—

do you believe him, with his face on loan
to imitate the learned and the just?
Try the faces of your friends; exalt *them*
to old disguises you can trust.

Poverty in the undecked bone may pay St. Francis.
Will the spending of our daily brittle coin
seem less counterfeit, or bear its weight,
when our faces with masters join?

No. This is your pallet of shortest straw,
your spine still aches upon a common beach.
These attitudes from glittering, pasted walls
stay properly out of reach;

and they are crumbling to your savage mold
faster than a diary adds the years.
No skill can save them long, or prop their beauty.
The lovely eyes seem split with tears.

Florence

7

The Death in Poems

The death in poems, the death in men,
no difference there, or margin much.
This poem will end like the shout of sex,
and be but paper signs to touch.

We are not real. Nor Neptune,
Perseus, the pantheon of fame.
I write these words and am relieved
and everything will stay the same.

Florence

8
Masaccio

No gorgeousness, no gracious wing,
no cherubs blowing out their cheeks,
no splendor, Solomon's dry hand,
no messenger who ever speaks.

This is no dream of loss and gain,
and penitence and suing grief.
Howling, stumbling to our world,
the tragic mouth, the comic leaf.

And man in need kneels on this wall,
and grateful woman receives her alms.
To be this human is enough:
with wounds and grace in face and palms.

Florence

9

To the Angel of the Annunciation

Come swiftly with folded arms for balance,
over the ground and not from glancing heaven;
come, not to startle, but report grave news,
as simple as two strangers met at noon.

She extends her palm for solace from brilliance.
Make no grand entrance to unhinge her reason.
Take one quick step beyond the portico,
no hurricane, no gazelle aflame with greeting.

Come like a pilgrim in mufti.
We are sick of noise and outlandish claims,
worn out with headlines and the mumming shadows.
One stride and you're in this world to a—

gasp deeper than pit or sullen mountain.
O there is no shelter in her shattered room—
the dumb enormous thresholds, the foot all light,
the angel, the angel, the angel!

Florence

10

Pietà

That turning where no faces mark the deed:
to be lifted up, up, beyond your name,
through the chill and heave of silent stars;

to be lifted, the ultimate weariness,
death, the white mother strong to gather you,
your many words dissolving like snow;

this is where we end—the cost enormous.
I see how the chisel has raked the skin,
I see the firm legs dwindling as they rise,

I see the mother and the ambitious son
fly all the grief they ever heeded.
We cannot see them now; nor guess their music.

Milan

FIVE

FOR KAREN

What do you carry that cannot be borne,
that even in your most graceful risings
your balance must waver, as now you stride
over thresholds, though your boyishness betrays,
the long heels threaten to spill you forward,
though your hard sweet bones soften to let life in?

Your true burdens are what I cannot see,
nothing like rock, nothing like bits of sky,
rather, a heaviness of gifts and favors,
until another season brings your beauty whole:
a woman, the future set calmly on her head,
like a figure poised homeward from a well.

And yet you tottered when you rose—
only as the inmost leaf tips toward light,
only as the brightest pool echoes shade—
yet tottered, and smiled, and stood. I say it outright:
it cannot be borne: the weight of life is cruel,
though you step like a dancer from this room.

A MAP TO YOUR HOUSE

I shan't read it; no, I much prefer
watching you sketch it large, sitting on our couch,
making clear what I had hoped would stay dense,
the roads, the parkways, to your innocence.

I hate maps; they demean the possible,
and grant but a handful of approaches.
This is too direct a way to meet your past;
whatever I find will be full of reproaches.

Verweile doch, said Faust, and set a theme
by which lovers, poets, drinkers dream.
But maps don't expect their contours to remain,
they'll shift their borders to suit a new terrain.

The map is done and neater than we needed.
X marks the final spot: *your* ground, *your* air.
How tiresome that reassembling, those objects
now imagined, then withdrawn. I shan't go there.

BLIND BIRD

What startles him? that he needs no eyes to look through,
that he still has eyes, but sees nothing?
that the scabs of his head, though soft enough to heal,
are too soft to front the world?

He'll never look at you, a-perch on his tinsel,
lids down like curtains closing for a dirge,
holding proof against any other waking,
the beauty he was blinded for.

Only touching truly sees. He's sick of sight;
he'd rather wait for hands to thread his silence,
for mouths one hundred eyes can't see.
Let him be—there's no more looking he would have.

from the painting by Morris Graves.

WHATEVER GOOD

Whatever good for art you did,
(and all that remains to be seen)
folding your long white legs away,
and, standing, brushing your skirt clean,

whatever good for art you did,
rising just in time, I still doubt
whether any blushless ode I've read
could ever match your maidenhead.

Marmorean, built for an age,
some sculpture might hold you in that dream;
no poem I know could stay you
standing, brushing your skirt clean.

Whatever good for art you did,
(and whoever said art must stay hid?)
only the centuries may show.
But the Muse, like you, gets up to go.

MAGDALENE READING

Elegant, frantic, surrendered, serious,
how should I seat her? Hands on her Holy Book,
folded in prayer, grieving, or as in La Tour,
palm to pensive cheek, sententious skull on lap?

That one's best. Van der Weyden's is too calm,
Piero di Cosimo's, a lady masking,
and Titian's Magdalene has no book at all—
only those Venetian breasts too big to hide.

La Tour's the one: that girl in profile,
in a brown study musing on despair,
a steady torch lifted from her weeping glass,
nude shoulder, hair straight down: you, my love.

TOURING

Crete. I've never been there. Your mouth's like Crete.
We set out–with the usual maps, direction-finders,
guessing at the deeps, careful of the shoals,
but no pretense to know where we were going,
a ship of fools like any two bodies or souls.

We sailed the rich Mediterranean,
the one without politics or war.
We invaded no one, nor stormed any shore,
showed no one passports, never changed coin;
the only custom we kept was closing our door.

Crete. Is it full of white boulders and sun?
The Minotaur's from Crete. I saw him burst
from his labyrinth to drink up the sea.
He drowned as we went past. He was jealous
of our loving; he hated our journey.

FACE

(They were not expected to invent Christ's face, as artistry
had invented Zeus or Osiris, but to retrieve it.) —Malraux

That means there *was* a Christ with a face, and I doubt it.
The artist who struggled with Son of Sam had an easier time
but still made a botch of it, neither finding nor creating,
but probably got closer than this first Romanesque attempt,
Tavant, 13th century, that neither invents nor retrieves.
Retrieval is the most impossible of human tasks.
Yesterday is gone, and I can't remember what you looked like,
so I go on inventing, retrieving to exhaustion,
doing you an injustice, doing you poorly.
When I kissed you, my face lingering on yours,
I might have had some idea of your features;
together we might have recovered part of what we were.
But you're gone as Zeus and Osiris are gone
and no more real than any Christ remaining.
I sit in foreign dark, feeling my face grow strange.

BLUEBEARD TO BEAUTY

All of my rooms are bloody
with no hero's blood at all–
I'd ask you in to kill you straight–
would anything appall?

I've dreamed of the soggy beard
and shrieked the red command–
I've sat to the nauseous meal,
toyed with the severed hand.

Seven rooms, beautiful girl,
excellent lady, Pain's the Place!
The whips are harmless, the rack's on rent
but let us dawdle for a space

and then to the armoury
where all my weapons rust
their sad incompetence
to bleed against the dust.

In the treasury you stop
to try a ruby at your throat;
it's a hunk of liver dyed
from the blood of a timid goat.

The garden's next–its gagging fern,
a plant like an ear; ear's plant;
a tongue in that ear, blood greening
out a soaking word–what did I want?

This, I wanted, and I have.
My domains you see stretched like a bride,
the soft piazza, the fountain,
the day bleeds down inside.

And we've come to the lake of tears.
That sludge is life's regrets—
for pain? for painful pleasure?
the lake of tears forgets.

For the ladies passing now
were really only poems.
I sent them away, without a verb,
to the bandages of homes.

We are walled, we are walled, Beauty—
the opera grinds another view.
Come into my empty room
heaped like a heart. I love you.

TO–

You came sliding from dream's-edge,
you showed your teeth as always,
poised, but moving, leant away.
It was you; it was not a dream:
in the halls, laughter at the edge,
in the doorway, hand smoothing hair.

Come closer; walk by me like thought—
no predicate, no answer,
staring from your salty distances!
But if it is you, don't stay long,
composing your beauty to need.
I know where you've been, where you are.

I can't afford your history.
In the door you fling your arms out
in two directions, both sad.
I think freely you have gone each way;
I glow at your courage.

Your hair has turned auburn.
You stand very still for my kiss.
I dream; it is not you I dream.

SIX

WE HAVE TO START SOMEWHERE

Bacchus, Jupiter, their busy childhoods,
and Tarzan too, an early riser, undoubtedly,
all of them quick off the mark, but does it help?
Kind women circling them, so many hands,
milky breasts, graceful, supportive arms
with light draperies falling like dreams,
and those landscapes! perfect in distance,
golden age where gods did sup and sprawl,
a Herm, a centaur, a pissing cherub . . .

It was easy to grow up then.
Bacchus from tipsy youth bloomed savagely,
Jupiter's nod swelled terribly with power,
and Tarzan, whom we better understand,
perfected his birth-shriek for decades

to an inescapable demand for attention.

FUNERAL HOME

1

The house was always faint with ruin,
and down the back stairs, in a sudden start,
you'd catch the drift of death, formaldehyde
and scrubbed enamel, and worn-out roses,
and rushing through the vestibule you tried
to give the house an easier heart
to breathe with than any breath disposes.

2

A lie, a lie. You loved it. It was your own:
the patient satin slits open like underwear,
the metal pricetags' dignified repose,
the quick unslatting of a hundred knees,
and the tiptoed giggling over the nose
of the dead man—when you heard the prayers
rise up like foghorns from agnostic seas.

3

But he kept still, with mouth never so shapely,
with hair never brushed so fine—like an ad.
And his glasses gave back no double thought;
you could trust him to stay Another's Wrong.
Except when, rising from the rail, you caught
his face, pallid as frozen lemonade,
and you drank him deep, the whole summer long.

4

The cars are here! Bumper to bumper, lovely,
each solemn door receives a solemn aunt,
and mourners go in orders perilous

to ride without expense; the sun fresh-stamps
a halo in each glass—console us!—
and each black flag assures there won't, there can't
be death, until God damps the votive lamps.

5

Downstairs, a stale despair. I read the names
signed in the book, looking for a spy;
I dust, and fold the chairs, and scrape the wax
and open the windows to let the moths fly out.
There are ash and mucus and spittle on the backs
of chairs; there is a bug who wants to die;
and a girl's ribbon, looking for a throat.

6

Younger, we crashed the empty casket trucks
across the polished floor like dodgems of our own.
I shinned Mike silly. Hiding in the hearse
was better than bush or musty shut-down barn!
But he spoiled it, broke a candle, and worse,
screwed little Lorraine Otash to the bone.
Does a hearse ride better when the corpse is warm?

7

The hill is at best a gradual slope;
the house sits on no manorial lawn;
the field was never a place of strenuous games;
the driveway hardly holds two cars.
Yet the moon would sometimes dust the panes
to a patience steadier than its own.
The cupola would lift, certain as the stars.

8

Only the mill-wheel's sound, the grasses thinning.
The drivers lean upon their doors, the bearers

feel their shoulders healing; the women tilt.
Everyone is propped; the priest is grinning.
And when they gravel home again, bearers,
drivers, women—what have they salvaged or spilt?
Only the mill-wheel's sound, the grasses thinning.

9

Once, startled on an entrance in, dumb
that any visitor had lodged (sign in, please!)
he shrieked and ran upstairs, and heard
this one had drowned and swelled the coffin tight.
That was the end—as though the savage Word
were out, and there would be no life to seize.
On the bed he lay like Echo, sobbing through the night.

10

Father, father, you expected so much.
Like Glad Day every dawn I'd leaped to pull
the mummies from their bandages of fright,
and spin gay quoits chancing through your halls...
Did you hear a dozen trucks in wreck last night?
Who will bury them? fill them full?
Burn the bodies in the street; this house appalls.

THE MILLIONAIRE'S SON

for Daniel Hughes Senior
1896-1975

1

I heard a man say, *we* are the life on Mars
and thought it a cunning solution.
We are the only life we bring anywhere,
but it's your death I'm bringing to this page.
I am your life then; I travel with two lives, one death,
and I never did before. I'm used to more ballast,
I'm in danger of floating away now,
your life does not weigh on me, your death is leaving.
I would be heavy with inheritance
but I'm too light in my life; my life's a cheap balloon.

2

Father, you are not hearing the Clarinet Concerto,
and you are not shaving or expecting company.
I am doing these things but because you are dead
I am fat with doubleness, I am double-bright.
I turn to my guests swollen with insight.

Father, there's a new weight in my doing.
Wisdom puffs my handshake; I seem to taste the wine twice.
You would have hated it and gulped it fast,
but, accomplished at last, I must *be* you.
Deep-voiced with meaning, I've never sounded so true.

Burly man, skinny man, you liked to fall on me,
and once I warned you I wouldn't catch you again.
You put your heels together and tilted toward me—
"No! I won't catch you, you'll fall, you'll slip—"
Hercules and grabbing Antaeus at grip,

Renaissance-style! and down we went in our weakness,
like partridges shot from the sky,
foolish, splat on the kitchen floor.
"For God's sake, get up! I'd thought you'd catch me. At least you'd try."

Why should we rise? Laugh, dead. Here let us lie.

3

You fell again—with an actor's despatch.
The millionaire's son wasn't there to catch you,
but the bounty of your gifts came pouring anyway.

Though light's your legacy and dark and any part of me,
I keep slinking from your charge.
We thought almost nothing as we fell to the floor.
This good day empties too. What was it for?

4

(1946)

"Aren't they going to get away, Dan, aren't they?"
No, there won't be a happy ending.
"Then why did I come to the movies,
and what does *Odd Man Out* mean? They should get away!"
But I knew good art never had a happy ending;
that was all I knew but I knew that—and smugged a smile.
We groused home, arguing about how things should come out.

I wonder still. Why did James Mason have to die?
Life, not art, will furnish forth catastrophes.
If I think ahead, I see ten thousand awful endings;
behind, there's the occluded, deceitful past.
We were afraid to tell the truth to each other:
Death is not a flash-point of wisdom,
death is not anything we will ever want to use.

Peak, then, blaze of being, this moment's fold!
My mind to me a holy city is
where you sit in its tallest, clearest councils.

If you are falling, you cannot fall further than myself.
Through these our mirrors, I catch you standing, whole.

TURN AWAY

Turn away, turn away,
walk away, walk away,
leave the severed head
in the middle of the field
where it brays at you and begs.
Turn away, turn away.

Like this: start to the right,
pivot slowly to savor the turn,
throw up your right hand,
use the left to sweep you round,
and there you are, away, away.
Nothing could have been easier.

You have left them behind you;
how quickly they grey and whimper
and forget their farewells.
Now they are wrappings, old shreds
never once for use or joy.
The void you enter is full of light.

Daniel Hughes lives in Detroit, Michigan where he teaches at Wayne State University. He has two previous volumes of poetry: *Waking in a Tree* and *Lost Tribe & Other Poems,* the latter published by Copper Beech Press in 1975.